Vikas Bhushan
A. R. D. Prasad

Linked Data: Legacy Data Discovery in Semantic Web Era

Vikas Bhushan
A. R. D. Prasad

Linked Data: Legacy Data Discovery in Semantic Web Era

LAP LAMBERT Academic Publishing

Impressum / Imprint
Bibliografische Information der Deutschen Nationalbibliothek: Die Deutsche Nationalbibliothek verzeichnet diese Publikation in der Deutschen Nationalbibliografie; detaillierte bibliografische Daten sind im Internet über http://dnb.d-nb.de abrufbar.
Alle in diesem Buch genannten Marken und Produktnamen unterliegen warenzeichen-, marken- oder patentrechtlichem Schutz bzw. sind Warenzeichen oder eingetragene Warenzeichen der jeweiligen Inhaber. Die Wiedergabe von Marken, Produktnamen, Gebrauchsnamen, Handelsnamen, Warenbezeichnungen u.s.w. in diesem Werk berechtigt auch ohne besondere Kennzeichnung nicht zu der Annahme, dass solche Namen im Sinne der Warenzeichen- und Markenschutzgesetzgebung als frei zu betrachten wären und daher von jedermann benutzt werden dürften.

Bibliographic information published by the Deutsche Nationalbibliothek: The Deutsche Nationalbibliothek lists this publication in the Deutsche Nationalbibliografie; detailed bibliographic data are available in the Internet at http://dnb.d-nb.de.
Any brand names and product names mentioned in this book are subject to trademark, brand or patent protection and are trademarks or registered trademarks of their respective holders. The use of brand names, product names, common names, trade names, product descriptions etc. even without a particular marking in this work is in no way to be construed to mean that such names may be regarded as unrestricted in respect of trademark and brand protection legislation and could thus be used by anyone.

Coverbild / Cover image: www.ingimage.com

Verlag / Publisher:
LAP LAMBERT Academic Publishing
ist ein Imprint der / is a trademark of
OmniScriptum GmbH & Co. KG
Heinrich-Böcking-Str. 6-8, 66121 Saarbrücken, Deutschland / Germany
Email: info@lap-publishing.com

Herstellung: siehe letzte Seite /
Printed at: see last page
ISBN: 978-3-659-75594-1

Zugl. / Approved by: Bangalore, Indian Statistical Institute, DRTC, Masters Dissertation, 2014

Acknowledgements

I am thankful to my guide Prof. A.R.D. Prasad for giving me ideas and suggestions, despite his busy schedule. I am expressing my deep and sincere gratitude towards him for the encouragement and the freedom I received, which in turn helped to complete my work with perfection.

I would like thank to Dr. Devika Madalli, Dr. Biswanath Dutta and Dr. B.S. Dayasagar and Dr. Saiful Amin, for their inspiring guidance and support in the due course.

I wish to express my deep sense of gratitude to our administrative staffs, especially, Mr. Kalyan Raman, for the much needed support in the institute which helped me in completing the project work in time.

Finally, I would like to express my gratitude to my parents for their blessings and support that helped me to overcome all the hurdles in my life, my seniors especially Mr. Subhashis Das, PhD student at University of Trento, Italy, my classmate Mr. Sayon Roy and to all our Research Scholars specially Mr. Anindaya Basu for their help in completing the project.

Lastly I would like to thanks Bangalore for its pleasant weather.

Table of Contents

List of Abbreviations

1. API: Application Programming Interface
2. CSV: Comma Separated Value
3. DERA: Domain, Entity, Relation, Attribute
4. KOS: Knowledge Organization System
5. LMF: Linked Media Framework
6. LOD: Linked Open Data
7. RDF: Resource Description Framework
8. RDFS: Resource Description Framework Schema
9. SKOS: Simple Knowledge Organization System
10. SPARQL: Simple Protocol And RDF Query Language
11. URI: Uniform Resource Identifier
12. OWL: Web Ontology Language

1   Introduction:

The evolution of Semantic Web from Syntactic Web has made data on the web machine processable. Despite all these progress made, one of the biggest challenge towards the use of semantics is the lack of background knowledge [1]. Capturing this background knowledge is a tough problem to deal with due to the nature of knowledge. Knowledge doesn't have one uniform description. Everyone has different perception of a particular knowledge; for instance, Rose as a flower, as a fragrance, as an actress, as a love etc. Also we cannot conclude any distance or relation between two entities as equidistant. And here we are trying to capture this multidimensional knowledge, which is vast in terms of size, continuum and dynamic in nature and has diverse sources [2]. Moreover, we want that it should be of high quality and contextually relevant.

For encountering this difficulty Giunchiglia [et al] has proposed and adapted the faceted approach, well-established methodology used in the field of Library science for knowledge organisation in Libraries [3] and came up with DERA, a new faceted knowledge representation approach [4]. This provides the solution for the development of Descriptive Ontologies, which allows scaling to the ever growing knowledge. DERA is faceted because it has its root in category-based systems and especially from the faceted approach given by Ranganathan (1967) and which was later simplified by Bhattacharyya (1975). However, it differs from them as it is entity-centric rather than document-centric and the original aims at the development of classification ontologies while this at descriptive ontologies, which can be formalised into description logic ontologies thus enabling automated reasoning. So, DERA methodology can be applied in building ontologies for domains, as evident from the papers on the subject [5].

But developing ontologies from scratch is an extremely time-consuming, costly, error prone task and it is therefore fundamental to reuse existing resources. This can be achieved by connecting or linking related concepts or entities from various datasets available as a giant network of interconnected resources, the Linked Open Data Cloud1. This enables different applications to interoperate and share their data. Thus enhancing reusability of our data and this sharing is increasing day by day, which is clearly visible from the growing size of the LOD cloud. However for integrating datasets, purpose should be taken into account and make explicit the semantics [6]. Typically it can be achieved by mapping between their terms/concepts.

1.1   Problem and Motivation:

We all understand the importance of data many a times and being a library and information science professional, our job is to make best use of raw data and to make it information. In this dynamic web environment role of the libraries are also changing, which made a renowned information scientist to say that "in a metaphorical sense, we are moving from a Ptolemaic world with the library at the centre to a Copernican one with information at the centre and the library as one of its planets" (Robert S. Taylor). The bibliographic data painstakingly created by libraries are highly-structured and of high quality. So, if we want to sustain i.e. to make our data visible, reusable and discoverable in present scenario, we have to make it machine processable. This can be attained by using Semantic Web techniques with Linked Data

---

[1] http://linkeddata.org/data-sets

principles. So, in this project an approach to apply these principles on the bibliographic data of our Hostel Library by annotating text using DBpedia Spotlight, tabular data using OpenRefine and publishing legacy data as Linked Data using Linked Media Framework has been taken. The basic assumption behind this is that there is increase in value and usefulness of datasets when interlinked with other data [7].

1.2   Structure of this document:

This dissertation is divided into seven sections. Dissertation begins with the introduction of the problem of discourse and motivation behind it. **Section 2** presents Semantic Web architecture with emphasis on Linked Data and its evolution, need, technology stack and working principles. The basic ingredient required for Linked Data like RDF for framework, vocabularies to describe data and SPARQL to make query. **Section 3** and **Section 4**, presents the State of Art and the preceding section show some of the emblematic use cases of Linked Data in general and in the succeeding section its application in context of Libraries. Next in **Section 5**, some of identified Open Research Issues related to Linked Data has been discussed. The **Section 6** will talk about the solution for annotating text as Linked Data and ways of publishing legacy data as Linked Data. Finally, **Section 7** will lead to conclusion of the work with future work and final remarks.

2   Semantic Web and Linked Data

This section will provide description of the Semantic Web. Here, Semantic means 'meaning' and Web means several documents, connected with each other via hyperlinks. These documents are web pages containing data, understandable and processable by humans. Whereas, Semantic Web means the meaningful web where data present in the web pages are also processable by machines. In this way machines would be able to interpret and understand the meaning of data in a web page and will present the user with needful information. Semantic Web as explained in the article by Tim Berners-Lee, James Hendler, and Ora Lassila, Scientific American, 2001 is as follows "The Semantic Web is not a separate Web but an extension of the current one, in which information is given well-defined meaning, better enabling computers and people to work in cooperation." [8]. So briefly, we can say that, the Semantic Web enables us to express data as well as rules for reasoning about the data.

2.1 Linked Data

Linked data is just addition of one more facet to the Semantic Web i.e. publishing and connecting data with related data [9]. So, we don't have to search for related concepts rather machine would provide it for us. This publishing of structured data on the Web is based on set of guiding principles, to interlink data making a Web of Documents to a Web of Data. In the following sub-sections, we will have the various aspects of Linked Data since its evolution to its working principles.

2.1.1 Evolution of Linked Data

The growth and development of the Linked Data can be traced way back with the invention of Web. Initially Web has the HTML pages with mainly made up of ASCII and images. It was syntactic in nature with human clickable hyperlinks which humans have to understand and then click to navigate from one page to other. This was popularly known as Web of documents. After this came the Semantic Web or Web 3.0, where data becomes machine processable. Now, machines can understand the data and able to understand Jaguar an animal and a car. Adding one more facet to Semantic Web i.e. connecting related data, gave birth to Linked Data. Thus forming the Web of Documents to Web of Data [10]. This can be represented in the form of below provided figure 1:

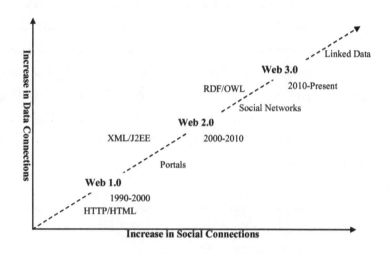

Figure 1: Stages of Linked Data evolution

2.1.2 Need for Linked Data

The rationale behind the Linked Data is the need for enhancing re-usability, findability and visibility of our data. In order to achieve this several approaches were adopted prime among them are Microformats and Web APIs. But they have some shortcoming like Microformats were meant to represent data about small set of various entities. Further, Web APIs were with vendor locked interfaces and most doesn't have global unique identifiers for entities, so we cannot set hyperlinks between entities of different Web APIs. Web APIs thus 'Slice the Web into separate data silos' making data sets isolated, unconnected but with Linked data related concepts can be joined, moreover machine would be able to do the processing.

2.1.3 Linked Data Working Principles

Linked Data working principles are a set of best practices that have been designed for publishing and interlinking related data on the web in a way that it becomes part of a unified global data set [11]. According to these rules by Tim Berners-Lee – every entity must have a Uniform Resource Identifier[2] (URI) that, when followed up should provide useful information, using the standards like RDF and SPARQL. Along with these, the entity must be linked to other related concepts so that more entities can be discovered. These principles can be depicted by given Figure 2 [12]:

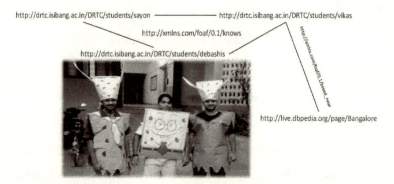

Figure 2: URIs for identifying people and the relationships between them

Now the principle says we must Use URIs as names for things, so here we represented people with URIs, then we must provide information

---

[2] http://isi.edu/in-notes/rfc2396.txt accessed on 1/06/2014

using standard like RDF, so here concepts are in the form of triples with Subject, predicate and Object.

Lastly it says to include links to other related entity, so that they can discover more things, so here we have linked it with location of the figure to get more related information. In the following sections, technologies needed to use Linked Data are described.

2.2 RDF

RDF is an acronym for Resource Description Framework, it is a standard defined by World Wide Web Consortium (W3C) for description of web resources. According to the W3C Semantic Web Activity Statement – The RDF is a language designed to support the Semantic Web, in a similar way as the HTML is the language that helped initiate the original web. It is a framework for supporting resource description, or metadata (data about data), for the Web. RDF gives common format that can be used for interoperable XML data exchange. RDF describes any bit of information on Web in a triple form using Subject, Predicate and an Object. RDF can be assumed as a directed graph having labeled nodes and arcs or as an object-oriented model having (object/attribute/value) [13]. This can be described by the provided Figure 3.

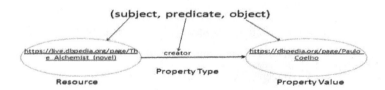

Figure 3: Graphical Representation of a RDF statement

The Subject of a triple is a resource about which we want to say and it must have a URI; predicate is the relationship between Subject and an Object and the Object is either a simple literal value for the resource or a URI of another resource which is somehow related to the subject. It has a variety of serialization formats, i.e., file formats (e.g., XML, Notation 3 (N3), N-Triples, Turtle (Terse RDF Triple Language), etc.). The goal is to make available information for the applications to process, rather than only for human consumption.

2.3   Vocabularies

In the Semantic Web context, vocabularies are used to define the resources and the relationships between them of domain of interest. These are the basic building blocks on the Semantic Web for inference ability. The purpose of vocabularies is to facilitate data integration when exist any ambiguity between terms used in various datasets. It is also used to organize knowledge in libraries, government portals etc. to harness the potential of Linked Data. The distinction between the term "vocabularies" and "ontologies" is not so clearly defined. The trend is we use the term "ontology" for more complex, and possibly quite formal collection of terms, whereas when such strict formalism is not required then "Vocabulary" is used[3].

2.3.1 Ontologies with OWL

The Web Ontology Language (OWL) is a language for Semantic Web that constitutes rich and complex knowledge about concepts, groups of concepts, and relations among them. It is based on computational logic such that knowledge expressed using this is reasoned by computer programs for checking the consistency of that

[3] http://www.w3.org/standards/semanticweb/ontology#summary retrieved on 02/06/2014

knowledge or to make semantics explicit. OWL documents are known as ontologies which can be published on Web and can be referred to or from another OWL ontologies4. It provides much richer vocabularies than XML, RDF, and RDF Schema along with formal semantics. OWL follows an object-oriented approach and it describes a domain in terms of classes and properties [14].

2.3.2 Controlled terminology with SKOS

The Simple Knowledge Organization System (SKOS) is a vocabulary that can be used with RDF to represent Knowledge Organization Systems (KOs) like thesauri, classification schemes, List of subject heading systems and taxonomies, which don't have explicit relations among terms. SKOS provides efficient and economical conversion path for semi-formal KOs to the Semantic Web [15]. As it is based upon RDF, representations are machine-processable and supports interoperability among software applications [16].

2.4 Querying with SPARQL

In Semantic Web context the term "Query" means technology and rules by which we can retrieve information programmatically from the Web of Data5. As in Semantic Web data is described using RDF so to retrieve stored data from RDF triple store, SPARQL is needed as a query language. It is similar to SQL in the sense that data stored in Relational Database Management Systems is retrieved via this. SPARQL facilitates sending and receiving queries via HTTP or SOAP. Queries in the SPARQL are based on the triple pattern of RDF and

---

4 http://www.w3.org/TR/2012/REC-owl2-primer-20121211/#Introduction retrieved on 02/06/2014
5 http://www.w3.org/standards/semanticweb/query retrieved on 02/06/2014

based on pattern matching of the triples it will return the resources [17]. SPARQL query form of Select type looks like this:

PREFIX a: <http://localhost/hostellibrary#>

SELECT ?x ?y

WHERE { ?x a:hascreator ?y }

Here, Prefix is the mechanism to abbreviate URI; Select provides variables to be returned and Where provides Query patterns (list of triple patterns).

2.5 Data Access Control

Data Access Control is a technique which enables an Agent (mainly HTTP server) to allow other Agents to carry out various activities on Resources according to the Access Control Graph of that Resource[6] i.e. which user can access the data. Data Access Control has become a necessity if we want to control who will access our data in the present Semantic Web environment. Several solutions have been proposed to address this issue of access control on data; most among them depends on the Access Control Graph. One among them is Relation Based Access Control model (RELBAC) proposed in [18], this is based on description logics to provide a permission model. The basic building blocks of this model are Subject, Object, Permissions and Rules. It has permission hierarchies, with permissions as relations between Subjects and Objects and the type of access rights that Subjects have on an Object is expressed by Rules.

---

[6] http://www.w3.org/2012/ldp/wiki/AccessControl retrieved on 02/06/2014

2.5.1 Linked Data Vs Linked Open Data

According to Tom Heath - Not all Linked Data will be open, and not all Open Data will be linked[7]. So there is an important difference between these two terms; Linked Data is the data which is linked with other related datasets but is not open to reuse whereas, the Linked Open Data is the data which is linked as well as published under an Open License to reuse. From figure 4[8], it's possible to see the graph of Linked Open Data as of September 2011.

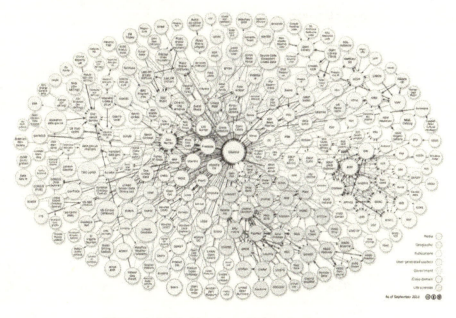

Figure 4: LOD Cloud as of September 2011

[7] http://linkeddata.org/faq retrieved on 02/06/2014
[8] Linking Open Data cloud diagram, by Richard Cyganiak and Anja Jentzsch. http://lod-cloud.net/ retrieved on 02/06/2014

3   Emblematic Use Cases of Linked Data

This section covers some of use cases and applications from library community and associated areas collected and analyzed by W3C Library Linked Data Incubator Group. These uses cases and case studies reflect the possible benefits of Linked Data technologies in describing Library resources with explicit Semantics and linking to related entities from other sources [19]. Almost all applications described use, one way or another DBpedia [20]. These use cases are classified into eight broader categories and the figure 5[9] depicts them:

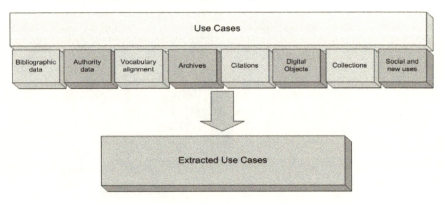

Figure 5: Use case Categorization

3.1   Bibliographic data

This category consists of use cases related to bibliographic records.

3.1.1 AGRIS

The AGRIS[10] (International Information System for the Agricultural Sciences and Technology) database aggregates and disseminates bibliographic references, such as research articles, findings and theses related to agricultural domain. Presently only a "trivial linking" of terms

---

[9] http://www.w3.org/2005/Incubator/lld/XGR-lld-usecase-20111025/UCReport-v1.png retrieved on 07/05/2014

[10] http://agris.fao.org/agris-search/index.do retrieved on 07/05/2014

has been done from the AGRIS record to specific Google searches [21]. In this way user searching on AGRIS database will get related information from other sources on the LOD.

3.2   Authority data

Libraries are moving fast from catalog cards to networked databases and from confined four walls to Web in order to serve its user better. Authority data plays a crucial role library data movements and its goal is to have collaborative use and maintenance of authority records of participating institutions, thus reducing occurrence of redundancies [22]. Some implementations in this regard are as follows:

3.2.1 Virtual International Authority File (VIAF)

VIAF[11] is a joint project of the Library of Congress, the Deutsche Nationalbibliothek, and the Bibliothèque nationale de France, with the cooperation of an increasing number of other national libraries across the world and various agencies, for virtually joining the name authority files of these organisations into a unified name authority service.

3.2.2 FAO Authority Description Concept Scheme

This project has been undertaken by Food and Agriculture Organization of the United Nations (FAO) with the aim to facilitate several multilingual forms of an entity by using URIs along with the relationships among them. It improves searching and access of the records due to the consistency in the forms employed to recognize

---

[11] http://oclc.org/research/activities/viaf.html retrieved on 07/05/2014

various concepts [23]. Figure 6[12] depicts how this has been used in FAO.

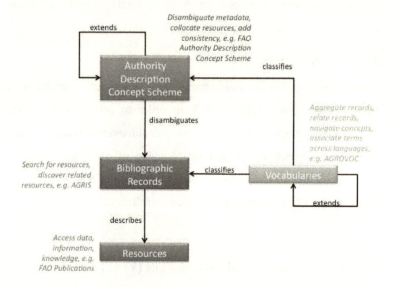

Relationships Between FAO Linked Data Use Cases

Figure 6: Use of FAO Authority Description Concept Scheme

3.3 Vocabulary alignment

Vocabulary heterogeneity in a domain gave rise to the need of vocabulary alignment, so that different sources having similar concepts could be retrieved.

3.3.1 AGROVOC Thesaurus

The AGROVOC Thesaurus is a multi-lingual terminology in agriculture, fisheries, food, forestry and related domains like environment of FAO. This has been implemented with SKOS concept

---

12

http://www.w3.org/2005/Incubator/lld/wiki/File:FAO_Relationships_between_Use_Cases.png retrieved on 07/05/2014

scheme and it enables tagging and discovering of research results from multiple languages. The expression of concepts as Linked Data facilitates in creation of explicit equivalence relations among AGROVOC terms and terms available in Vocabularies of agriculture in other data-sets. Figure 7[13] depicting interface of AGROVOC Thesaurus.

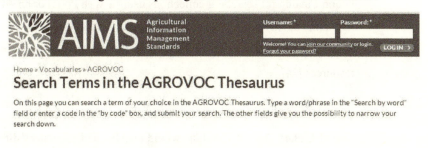

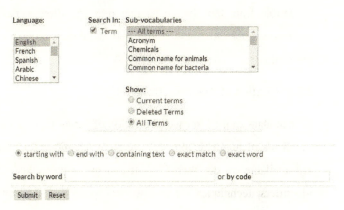

Figure 7: AGROVOC Thesaurus search interface

3.4   Archives and heterogeneous data

Linked Data and Semantic Web techniques are adopted in maintaining Archives to attain semantic connections with related concepts leading to serendipitous discovery of resources for users and better data management for participating institutions.

---

[13] http://aims.fao.org/standards/agrovoc/functionalities/search retrieved on 07/05/2014

3.4.1 Europeana

Europeana[14] provides service across Europe by aggregating metadata from libraries, museums, archives, and audio-visual contents. It acts as a Union Catalog for searching collections using a Web Portal or an API. It has aim of harvesting resource metadata and links to resources, describing the resources explicitly and finally providing access to these resources [24].

3.5   Citations

Use of Linked Data in Citations would enable cited references directly accessible from the citation so that user can directly navigate to the referenced publication and would also facilitate automatic evaluation of publications.

3.5.1 Citation of Scientific Datasets

Linked Data applied in case of Citation of Scientific datasets will end to the chaos of non-availability of de-facto technique for citing data that are available on the Web [25]. It can guide in method for assigning identifiers, techniques for linking data, providing description of data, creators and publications with the use of vocabularies. This will enable automated systems to extract data and compute credit measures for the authors automatically.

3.6   Digital objects

3.6.1 LUCERO project

Linking University Content for Education and Research Online (LUCERO)[15] project has the aim of aggregating contents related to

---

[14] http://www.europeana.eu/ retrieved on 07/05/2014
[15] http://kmi-web06.open.ac.uk/lb/ retrieved on 10/05/2014

courses at The Open University[16] [26]. Presently if a student, lecturer or a researcher wants to search for resources like books, CDs, articles, Podcasts, TV program, Open Educational Resources, etc. related to a specific Open University course then have to search at different data sources available at different interfaces for each type of document required, explore them and then manually integrate the results. This project has the following goals:

o SEARCH/BROWSE: This will enable a student to provide a interface where all the resources related to the course along with supplementary documents will be available at one place i.e. all the related resources will be brought together from different data sources.

o URIS, RELATE (new, existing), REUSE-SCHEMAS (SKOS): The resources such as people, courses, topics and publications should play a central role in linking Open University datasets to each other, and to external related concepts. This should enhance reuse by different department needing same resource.

3.7 Collections

3.7.1 AuthorClaim

AuthorClaim[17] is an application that has been designed for identifying person responsible for a particular work i.e. author, editors, and contributors as recorded in a bibliographic database. Here, document metadata records are classified by subject experts and they make a binary decision about a resource whether it belongs to a category or not. The result is a document collection forming an issue of a subject report.

---

[16] http://www.open.ac.uk/ retrieved on 10/05/2014
[17] http://authorclaim.org/ retrieved on 10/05/2014

Linked Data techniques are applied here to reuse data from other available data sources and to export the profiles, with bibliographic information as used in AuthorClaim along with the original bibliographic records.

3.8   Social and new uses

The social web or web 2.0 is becoming an essential part of life. One of the important duties of a library is to promote community building, and there is capability for building this around documents and other resources online. Further, taking advantage of social media libraries can use this community for its own benefits. This covers the social and the emergent / new uses of library information in the social web [27].

3.8.1 Crowdsourced Catalog

In case of Crowdsourced Catalog, Linked Data technologies are used for improving and enhancing library records or even creating new records by providing bibliographic data to volunteers. Through this type of initiatives library records can be refined at no extra cost and further the resulting library records could be made available as Open Data and therefore be available for wider use [28]. Some of existing works are as follows:

- o Biblios.net[18]
- o Flickr Commons[19]
- o Librarything[20]
- o Open Library[21]

---

[18] http://biblios.net/ retrieved on 11/05/2014
[19] https://www.flickr.com/commons/ retrieved on 11/05/2014
[20] https://www.librarything.com/ retrieved on 11/05/2014
[21] https://openlibrary.org/ retrieved on 11/05/2014

4 Linked Data in Libraries

Use of Linked Data in Libraries can be sub divided into following groups.

4.1 Classification systems

4.1.1 Dewey Decimal Classification (DDC)

DDC[22] uses Linked Data principles to provide its data as a small "terminology service". DDC has used these principles to assign URIs, not only for single classes but for every concept and these could be dereference back to obtain information about concepts in both human-readable as well as machine processable. Data can be accessed through SPARQL endpoints and will be reusable for non-commercial purposes under Creative Commons license. Its classification semantics are encoded using SKOS and are available in different serialization formats (RDF/XML, Turtle, JSON) [29].

4.1.2 Universal Decimal Classification (UDC)

The Universal Decimal Classification (UDC) is a multilingual classification scheme for all fields of knowledge with sophisticated indexing and retrieval mechanism. UDC Summary data is available in SKOS (XML/RDF) format. Linked Data has been used to interlink and make cross-references to make it more useful for both humans and computers. UDC linked data[23] along with UDC SKOS scheme[24] is available for download.

---

[22] http://dewey.info/ retrieved on 20/05/2014
[23] http://udcdata.info/udcsummary-skos.zip retrieved on 20/05/2014
[24] http://udcdata.info/udc-scheme retrieved on 20/05/2014

4.2 Subject headings/subject authority files

4.2.1 Library of Congress Subject Headings (LCSH)

LCSH has extensive list of subject headings available in print as well as Linked Data. Subject authority headings can be accessed through the Library of Congress Authorities and Vocabularies service[25].

4.3 Thesauri

4.3.1 Eurovoc

Eurovoc[26] is a multilingual, multidisciplinary thesaurus which covers activities of the European Union, the European Parliament in particular. It covers terms in 24 languages.

4.4 WordNet 3.0

WordNet[27] is a lexical database of English language for nouns, verbs, adjectives and adverbs which are grouped as a collection of Synsets (Cognitive synonym). Linked Data principles have been applied to interlink Synsets using conceptual-semantic and lexical relation between them. Its Linked Data version has been published by the Vrije Universiteit Amsterdam.

4.5 WorldCat – OCLC

OCLC WorldCat[28] uses Linked Data principles to make its catalog records available through search engines like Google. This has been done by mapping its records with the schema developed by Schema.org and launched by Google, Bing, Yahoo to create and support

[25] http://id.loc.gov/ retrieved on 20/05/2014
[26] http://eurovoc.europa.eu/drupal/ retrieved on 20/05/2014
[27] http://wordnetweb.princeton.edu/perl/webwn retrieved on 20/05/2014
[28] http://www.worldcat.org/ retrieved on 20/05/2014

a common set of schemas for structured data mark-up on web pages [30].

4.6   BIBFRAME – Library of Congress

BIBFRAME[29] is a project undertaken by the Library of Congress to better accommodate the future requirements of Library community. Major focus of the initiative will be to determine a transition path for the MARC 21 exchange format to more Web based, Linked Data standards [31].

5   Open Research Issues

The advent of Linked Data technologies had triggered the journey towards Web of Data from Web of Documents [10]. Still in order to accomplish the dream of using the web like a single global database needs to overcome various challenges like:

5.1   Link Maintenance

The quantity of resources on web is not static, rather dynamic in nature. So, is the case with the resources available as Linked Data. They are either updated; deleted or even new resources are added. In Linked Data, the concepts are mapped with the related concepts in other data sources, so if the concept with which our data has been mapped is deleted or added then it leads to dead link pointing at URI that does not exist or if new related resources added with different URIs then links between them is not being established. This can lead to the failure of whole Linked Data concept. So, such problems can be overcome by periodically recalculating links using frameworks like Silk [32] or

---

[29] http://bibframe.org/ retrieved on 25/05/2014

LinQL [33] by pointing to data sources that publish feeds, or by having subscription of central registries like Ping the Semantic Web[30] that keeps watch on addition or alteration in data.

5.2   Licensing

In the Semantic Web environment as data are both human-readable and machine processable. More and more applications are being developed to consume data present on the web. This demands explicit specification about the terms and conditions under which consumed data can be reused. This is needed to encourage the data providers to take part in the Web of Data and persuade the data consumers that they are not violating any rights of others by consuming data, needs an appropriate framework for publishing data [9]. To solve such issues, Creative Commons[31] has taken initiatives by providing open licensing framework for Creative works. This allows data providers to share data choosing from wide-range of options from "all rights reserved" to "some rights reserved".

5.3   Privacy

Linked Data has the vision of using web like a single global database [9]. This has merits in several ways but at the same time has some demerits also, such as the issue of privacy of data arising due to the linking with several related other sources. This issue requires to be handled by both technical and legal means along with awareness among the data providers about which data to link in what context. In this regard a remarkable work has been done by Weitzer on Information accountability [34].

---

[30] http://www.programmableweb.com/api/ping-the-semantic-web retrieved on 27/04/2014
[31] http://creativecommons.org/ retrieved on 29/05/2014

5.4 User Interfaces and Interaction Paradigms

The interface for users to interact with an application plays a vital role in the success or failure of a technology so this should be designed keeping in mind ease of access for the users. The important benefit of this technology from the user's aspect is the retrieval of related data from various sources at single place, though it appears to them that data comes from a single source. The applications discussed in the Section of use case are the success stories of this. Like hypertext browsers allowing users to navigate forward and backward across the web documents, similar interfaces must be provided in the Linked Data applications.

5.5 Trust, Quality and Relevance

In the Linked Data environment data comes from several sources, so in this type of situation the trustworthiness and quality of data is an important issue to overcome. Christian Bizer et al [35] have proposed an approach to deal with this problem, based on heuristically rating techniques for the trustworthiness, quality and relevance of data. Further, the problem of representing the trustworthiness of data obtained from several sources into a unified view in an interface is a vital challenge. In this regard not much work has been done yet, but the contribution like WIQA [35] and InferenceWeb [36] would be able to provide explanation about the quality and trustworthiness of data.

6 Proposal

This project intends to propose an approach to apply the principles of Linked Data on the bibliographic data of Indian Statistical

Institute Hostel Library, by annotating text using DBpedia Spotlight and publishing legacy data as Linked Data using OpenRefine and Linked Media Framework. Finally it concludes with comparison of used technique with an automatic conversion tool i.e. Csv2Rdf on same data set and need for Linked Data in general with particular emphasis for Libraries.

6.1   Requirements

This project is based on the use of Open Source Software to accomplish the desired goal of annotating text and linking legacy data. The software used are as follows:

> ### DBpedia Spotlight

DBpedia Spotlight[32] is a tool which can automatically annotate mentions of DBpedia resources in text, thus it provides a solution for mapping unstructured information sources to the LOD via DBpedia, Freebase, Schema.org and Customized SPARQL endpoints [37]. It recognizes names of resources or entities provided (e.g. "Paulo Coelho"), and subsequently matches it to unique identifiers (eg.dbpedia: Paulo coelho).

> ### RESTClient

RESTClient[33] is an add-on for the Web-browser that supports all HTTP methods like GET, POST etc. Through this we can execute requests and inspect their responses before diving into implementing it.

---

[32] https://github.com/dbpedia-spotlight/dbpedia-spotlight/wiki retrieved on 10/05/2014
[33] http://restclient.org/ retrieved on 10/05/2014

> **Google Refine 2.5**

Google Refine[34] is a free, open source, power tool used for cleaning messy data and linking it to databases like Freebase, DBpedia, Europeana etc with the help of respective SPARQL endpoints. It supports several import and export formats:

- Import: CSV, RDF/XML , Notation3
- Export: CSV, Excel, HTML Table , RDF/XML

It is available for Windows, Linux and Mac based operating systems.

> **Linked Media Framework 2.2.0**

Linked Media Framework[35] is a server application which supports central Semantic Web technologies such as:

- LMF Core: This has the Linked Data Server that allows exposing data following the Linked Data Principles.
- LMF Modules: It is used to extend the functionality of the Linked Media Server.

LMF can be used in publishing Legacy Data as Linked Data and building Semantic Search over Data.

---

[34] https://code.google.com/p/google-refine/ retrieved on 10/05/2014
[35] http://semanticweb.org/wiki/Linked_Media_Framework retrieved on 10/05/2014

6.2   Solution Architecture for Linking Legacy Data

To implement the project bibliographic data from the Hostel Library is collected. Data which is in plain text format will be annotated using DBpedia Spotlight by mapping the concepts with the available data-sets on LOD as mentioned in section 6.1 with the respective SPARQL endpoints. We can inspect the backend process using the RESTClient. For data available in CSV format we will imported into the Google Refine and the concepts are mapped with the desired data-set. This process of mapping data-sets in Google Refine is known as reconciliation service. Mostly this reconciliation will happen automatically, sometimes manual checking is required if there is any ambiguity due to polysemy and homonymy by opening the hyperlinks and verifying which sense of the Concept is required for the project. After this, data in columns are described and relationship between them is explicitly established with standard vocabularies in the triple form as Subject, Object and Predicate. Finally, data is exported in the required format. Finally, it is published using Linked Media Framework. The project data is desired in the pattern as shown in the figure 8:

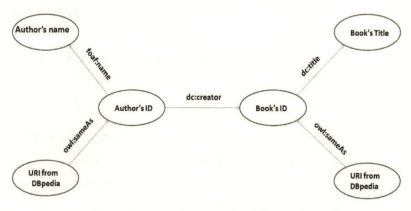

Figure 8: RDF Graph of the project

6.2.1 Annotating Text as Linked Data using DBpedia-Spotlight & RESTClient

Annotation of text using DBpedia-Spotlight and inspecting the backend process using RESTClient can be shown using following steps represented in pictorial manner:

- Step 1:Plain text data is entered into the DBpedia Spotlight[36]

Confidence:

0.5

Language: English

n-best candidates

SELECT TYPES...   ANNOTATE

Richard Bach is author of Jonathan Livingston Seagull

This demo uses the statistical DBpedia Spotlight web service at http://spotlight.sztaki.hu:2222/rest (how to cite).

---

[36] Joachim Daiber, Max Jakob, Chris Hokamp, Pablo N. Mendes Improving Efficiency and Accuracy in Multilingual Entity Extraction. Proceedings of the 9th International Conference on Semantic Systems (I-Semantics). Graz, Austria, 4–6 September 2013.

- Step 2: Selecting type of data-set to annotate

- Step 3: Finally, annotated text is obtained by clicking "Annotate" button

Next, for inspecting about the backend process using RESTClient following text is entered:

- "http://spotlight.dbpedia.org/rest/annotate?text=Richard%2 0Bach%20is%20author%20of%20jonathan livingston seagull.&confidence=0.2&support=20"

Confidence instructs DBpedia Spotlight to avoid incorrect annotations as much as possible at the risk of losing some correct ones and the support parameter, specify the minimum number of in links a DBpedia resource has to have in order to be annotated.

- Step 4: Entering text into RESTClient interface

- Step 5: Annotated text is displayed with other backend information

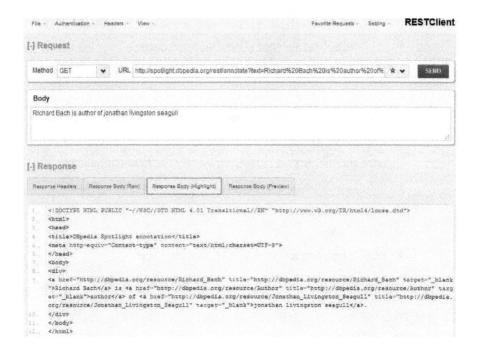

6.2.2 Publishing Legacy Data as Linked Data using:

Data available in tabular form can be linked to related data-sets available on LOD using following below mentioned techniques:

> **OpenRefine & Linked Media Framework**

Data in CSV format in this project can be reconciled and then published can be explained using following steps:

- Step 1: Bibliographic Data is imported into Google Refine

ID1	Authors	ID2	Book Title	Author.Id	Book.Id
1	Robert Silverberg	1	Passengers (short story)	1	1
2	Bill Bryson	2	A Short History of Nearly Everything	2	2
3	Roger Zelazny	3	Lord of Light	3	3
4	Samuel Beckett	4	Endgame (play)	4	4
5	Isaac Bashevis Singer	5	Shosha (novel)	5	5
6	Jose Saramago	6	Seeing (novel)	6	6
7	Jose Saramago	7	Blindness (novel)	7	7
8	Mario Vargas Llosa	8	The Way to Paradise	8	8
9	Daphne du Maurier	9	Jamaica Inn (novel)	9	9
10	Hunter S. Thompson	10	Fear and Loathing in Las Vegas	10	10
11	F. Scott Fitzgerald	11	The Great Gatsby	11	11
12	Washington Irving	12	Rip Van Winkle	12	12
13	Jim Corbett	13	Man-Eaters of Kumaon	13	13
14	John Irving	14	The Hotel New Hampshire	14	14
15	Ernest Hemingway	15	The Complete Short Stories of Ernest Hemingway	15	15
16	Chetan Bhagat	16	Five Point Someone – What not to do at IIT!	16	16
17	Ayn Rand	17	The Fountain Head	17	17
18	Haruki Murakami	18	Kafka on the Shore	18	18
19	Agatha Christie	19	The Body in the Library	19	19
20	Orhan Pamuk	20	Agatha Christie The mouse trap	19	20
21	Yasunari Kawabata	21	The Big Four (novel)	19	21
22	Ralph Ellison	22	My Name Is Red	20	22
23	John Updike	23	The Black Book (Pamuk novel)	20	23
24	Novels by Markus Zusak	24	The New Life	20	24
25	Jostein Gaarder	25	Snow (novel)	20	25

- Step 2: Reconciliation service is added to annotate it against related data-sets

- Step 3: SPARQL based reconciliation service added and initiated.

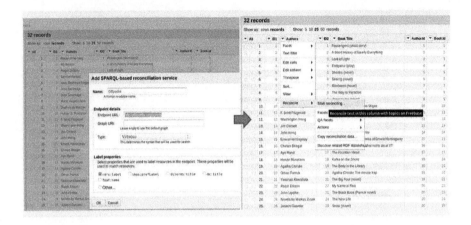

- Step 4: Reconciliation against DBpedia writer Ontology

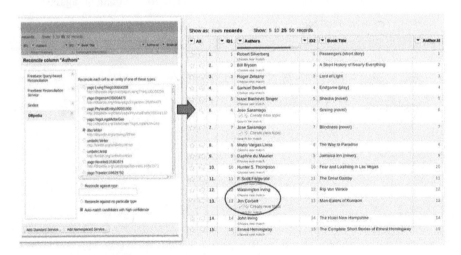

- Step 5: Concepts with ambiguity, needs manual matching

- Step 6: Creating Column for Author's URI after completion of reconciliation

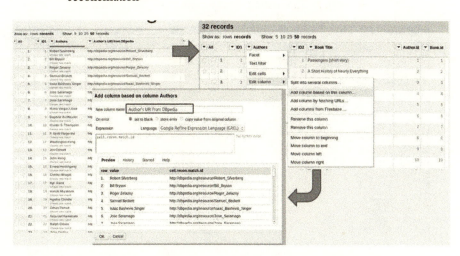

Similarly done for Book Title also.

- Step 7: Editing RDF Skeleton to obtain desired RDF Graph of the project

- Step 8: Eliminating Empty cells in Author's column

This step is required if number of authors is less than number of books.

- Step 9: Configuring Triples i.e. Subject, Predicate and Object using Vocabularies.

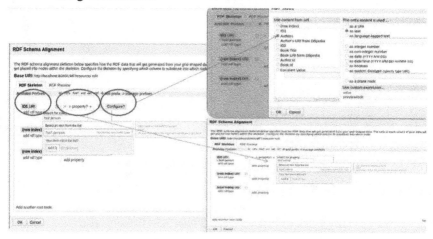

In similar manner this Step is repeated for Author's ID and Book ID.

- Step 10: Final RDF Skeleton of the Project

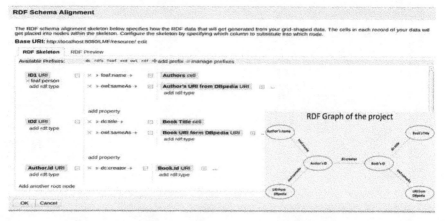

In right hand corner is the proposed graph of the project.

- Step 11: RDF Preview of Skeleton

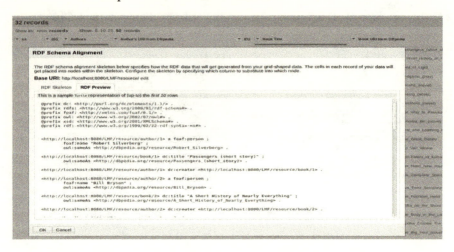

- Step 12: Data is exported in desired format i.e. RDF/XML

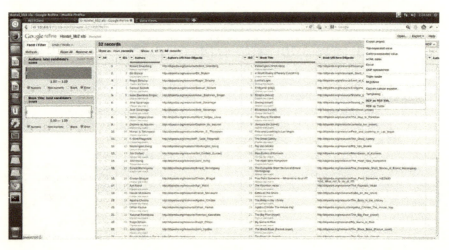

- Step 13: View of Exported RDF/XML

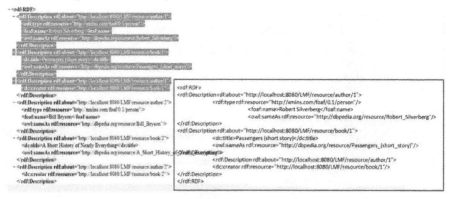

- Step 14: Publishing Data using LMF by importing our XML/RDF form of the data upload facility of LMF.

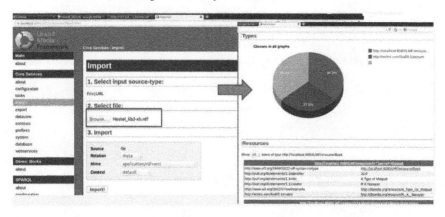

The pie-chart reflects that in uploaded data 36.2 % is the book title, 27.6% authors and rest are author's id and book id.

- Step 15: View of resource in triple form

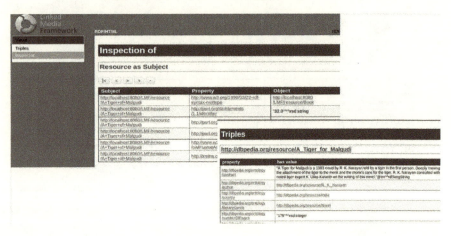

Here we get Subject, property and Object type relationship. If we click on subject we will get related or linked information about this book like:

- o Identifier which means book id
- o Abstract of the book
- o Country of Origin
- o Genre of the book, number of pages etc.

- Step 16: Now if we want to have related data/linked data about a single book then using rest client it will look like this:

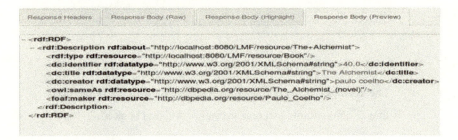

> **Csv2rdf converter**

Annotating the text using Csv2rdf, an automatic conversion tool can be show using below provided steps with figures:

- Step 1: Copying link location of CSV file from Hostel Library website

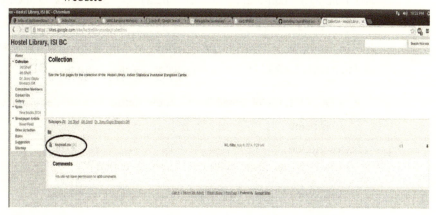

- Step 2: Providing address of CSV file

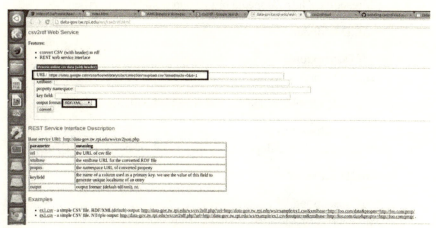

After this output RDF/XML file is generated and we can publish it in similar manner using LMF.

6.3   Evaluation methodology

The evaluation of the proposed project will be done by comparing the output files of both the adopted techniques for annotating tabular form of data obtained from Hostel Library in CSV format. We will examine each output by considering the fact better the Semantics explicitly described using standard Vocabularies like OWL, FOAF, Dublin Core etc. efficiently the data can be processed by machines. So, that machine can fetch more Linked Data to a concept or resource from the LOD.

- RDF/XML file obtained from Google Refine for a single resource is as below:

```
<rdf:Description
rdf:about="http://localhost:8080/LMF/resource/author/1">

    <rdf:type rdf:resource="http://xmlns.com/foaf/0.1/person"/>

    <foaf:name>Robert Silverberg</foaf:name>

    <owl:sameAs
rdf:resource="http://dbpedia.org/resource/Robert_Silverberg"/>

</rdf:Description>

<rdf:Description
rdf:about="http://localhost:8080/LMF/resource/book/1">

    <dc:title>Passengers (short story)</dc:title>

    <owl:sameAs
rdf:resource="http://dbpedia.org/resource/Passengers_(short_story)"/>

</rdf:Description>

<rdf:Description
rdf:about="http://localhost:8080/LMF/resource/author/1">

    <dc:creator
rdf:resource="http://localhost:8080/LMF/resource/book/1"/>
```

```
</rdf:Description>
```

- RDF/XML file obtained from Csv2rdf for a single resource is as below:

```
<rdf:Description rdf:about="#entry00001">

<rdf:type rdf:resource="http://data-gov.tw.rpi.edu/2009/data-gov-twc.rdf#DataEntry"/>

 <id1>1</id1>

 <authors>Robert Silverberg</authors>

 <id2>1</id2>

 <book_title>Passengers (short story)</book_title>

<author_id>1</author_id>

 <book_id>1</book_id>

 </rdf:Description>
```

7   Conclusion

This book addresses a vital issue about the nature of data and investigated into several techniques to handle this in the Semantic Web era. In this dynamic web environment role of the libraries are also changing, which made a renowned information scientist to say that in a metaphorical sense that earlier library used to be at the center and information used to revolve around it but in present web environment information acts as a focus point and libraries need to revolve around it, so as to full fill the information need of its patrons. The bibliographic data painstakingly created by libraries are highly-structured and of high quality. So, to make our data visible, reusable and discoverable in present scenario, we have to make it machine processable following Semantic Web techniques with Linked Data principles. The development in this regard is visible from the increasing number of data-sets available on LOD since its inception in 2007 to 2011 and from various applications developed following Linked Data principles.

Applying these Linked Data principles on bibliographic data of the Hostel Library to bring related data available on the LOD by annotating text using DBpedia Spotlight, tabular data using OpenRefine and publishing legacy data as Linked Data using Linked Media Framework has been taken. Finally a comparison between the two used techniques has been drawn after examining the Output RDF/XML files from both the used techniques for annotating tabular data in CSV format of the Hotel Library; that the RDF/XML files generated by Google Refine though semi-automatic i.e. need human intervention if any ambiguity arises due to polysemy and homonymy but is rich in Semantics as it is better described using standard Vocabularies. Whereas, the RDF/XML file generated by the Csv2rdf lacks the use of standard Vocabularies for describing the resource. So, it can be concluded that the machine can process and infer things to fetch Linked Data from LOD in a better way on result set obtained from Google Refine.

8   References:

[1] Giunchiglia, F. Dutta, B. Maltese, V. (2011). Domains and context: first steps towards managing diversity in knowledge. DISI Università di Trento, Trento, Italy

[2] Maltese, V. Giunchiglia, F. Denecke, K. Lewis, P. Wallner, C. Baldry, A. Madalli, D. (2009). On the interdisciplinary foundations of diversity

[3] S. R. Ranganathan. (1967) Prolegomena to library classification, Asia Publishing House

[4] Giunchiglia, F. Dutta, B. Maltese, V. (2013). From Knowledge Organization to Knowledge Representation

[5] Giunchiglia, F. Dutta, B. Maltese, V. Farazi, F. (2012). A facet-based methodology for the Construction of a Large-Scale Geospatial Ontology. Journal of Data Semantics. 1(1), 57-73

[6] Maltese, V., Farazi, F. (2011). Towards the Integration of Knowledge Organization Systems with the Linked Data Cloud. UDC seminar

[7] Chris Bizer, Richard Cyganiak, and Tom Heath. How to publish linked data on the web, 2007

[8] Tim Berners-Lee, James Hendler, and Ora Lassila. The semantic web.Scientific American, 284(5):34–43, 2001

[9] Christian Bizer, Tom Heath, and Tim Berners-Lee. Linked data - the story so far. International Journal on Semantic Web and Information Systems, 2009.

[10] Tom Heath and Christian Bizer. Linked Data: Evolving the Web into a Global Data Space. Morgan & Claypool, 1st edition, 2011.

[11] Tim Berners-Lee. Linked Data – Design Issues, 2006.

[12] Bhushan, Vikas (2014). Linked Data: Emblematic applications on Legacy Data in Libraries. In: Proceedings of the 17th National Convention on Knowledge, Library and Information Networking (NACLIN 2014), India (pp. 8-20).

[13] Jonathan Hayes. A graph model for rdf, 2004.

[14] X.H. Wang, D.Q. Zhang, T. Gu, and H.K. Pung. Ontology based context modeling and reasoning using owl. In Pervasive Computing and Communications Workshops, 2004. Proceedings of the Second IEEE Annual Conference on, pages 18–22, March 2004.

[15] SKOS Simple Knowledge Organization System Primer, W3C Working Group Note 18 August 2009. Retrieved from "http://www.w3.org/TR/skos-primer" on 22/05/2014

[16] SKOS Simple Knowledge Organization System Reference, W3C Working Group Note 18 August 2009. Retrieved from "http://www.w3.org/TR/skos-reference" on 22/05/2014

[17] SPARQL Query Language for RDF, W3C Recommendation 15 January 2008. Retrieved from "http://www.w3.org/TR/2008/REC-rdf-sparql-query-20080115/" on 02/06/2014

[18] Fausto Giunchiglia, Rui Zhang, and Bruno Crispo. Ontology driven community access control. In In SPOT2009 - Trust and Privacy on the Social and Semantic Web.

[19] Library Linked Data Incubator Group: Use Cases, W3C Incubator Group Report 25 October 2011. Retrieved from "http://www.w3.org/2005/Incubator/lld/XGR-lld-usecase-20111025/ "on 07/05/2014.

[20] Sören Auer, Christian Bizer, Georgi Kobilarov, Jens Lehmann, and Zachary Ives. Dbpedia: A nucleus for a web of open data. In In 6th Int'l Semantic Web Conference, Busan, Korea, pages 11–15. Springer, 2007.

[21] Use Case AGRIS, W3C Incubator Group Report 19 October 2010. Retrieved from "http://www.w3.org/2005/Incubator/lld/wiki/Use_Case_AGRIS" on 07/05/2014.

[22] Cluster Authority data, W3C Incubator Group Report 11 September 2011. Retrieved from "www.w3.org/2005/Incubator/lld/wiki/Cluster_Authority_data" on 07/05/2014.

[23] Use Case FAO Authority Description Concept Scheme, W3C Incubator Group Report 15 October 2010. Retrieved from "http://www.w3.org/2005/Incubator/lld/wiki/Use_Case_FAO_Au thority_Description_Concept_Scheme" on 07/05/2014

[24] Use Case Europeana, W3C Incubator Group Report 11 August 2011 retrieved from "www.w3.org/2005/Incubator/lld/wiki/Use_Case_Europeana" on 08/05/2014.

[25] Christine L. Borgman. 2010. "Research Data: Who will share what, with whom, when, and why?" China-North America Library Conference, Beijing Available at: http://works.bepress.com/borgman/238

[26] Use Case collecting material related to courses at The Open University, W3C Incubator Group Report 26 November 2010 retrieved from "http://www.w3.org/2005/Incubator/lld/wiki/Use_Case_Collecting_material_related_to_courses_at_The_Open_University" on 10/05/2014

[27] Uldis Bojārs and Jodi Schneider. 2011. Cluster Social Uses. Available at: http://www.w3.org/2005/Incubator/lld/wiki/Cluster_Social_Uses on 10/05/2014

[28] Use Case Crowdsourced Catalog, W3C Incubator Group Report 30/03/2011 retrieved from www.w3.org/2005/Incubator/lld/wiki/Use_Case_Crowdsourced_Catalog on 11/05/2014.

[29] Dewey Summaries as Linked Data, retrieved from "http://www.oclc.org/en-US/dewey/webservices.html" on 20/05/2014.

[30] Data Strategy and Linked Data, retrieved from "http://www.oclc.org/data.en.html" on 20/05/2014.

[31] Eric Miller, Uche Ogbuji, Victoria Mueller, and Kathy MacDougall. Bibliographic Framework as a Web of Data:Linked Data Model and Supporting Services, Library of Congress, 2012 retrieved from "http://www.loc.gov/bibframe/pdf/marcld-report-11-21-2012.pdf on 25/05/2014.

[32] Robert Isele, Anja Jentzsch, Chris Bizer, and Julius Volz. Silk - A Link Discovery Framework for the Web of Data, January 2011.

[33] O. Hassanzadeh, L. Lim, A. Kementsietsidis, and M. Wang. A Declarative Framework for Semantic Link Discovery over Relational Data. In Proceedings of the 18th International World Wide Web Conference (WWW2009), page 231, April 2009.

[34] Daniel J. Weitzner, Harold Abelson, Tim Berners-Lee, Joan Feigenbaum, James A. Hendler, and Gerald J. Sussman. Information accountability. Commun. ACM, 51(6):82–87, 2008.

[35] Christian Bizer and Richard Cyganiak. Quality-driven information filtering using the wiqa policy framework. J. Web Sem., 7(1):1–10, 2009.

[36] Deborah L. McGuinness and Paulo Pinheiro da Silva. Infrastructure for web explanations. In Dieter Fensel, Katia Sycara, and John Mylopoulos, editors, The Semantic Web — ISWC 2003, pages 113–129, 2003.

[37] Pablo N. Mendes , Max Jakob , Andrés García-Silva , Christian Bizer, DBpedia spotlight: shedding light on the web of documents, Proceedings of the 7th International Conference on Semantic Systems, p.1-8, September 07-09, 2011, Graz, Austria.

Appendix A: List of figures

Today, in web based environment we are surrounded by data. And we all understand the importance of data at many a times. So, if we want to sustain i.e. to make our data visible & discoverable in present scenario, we have to make our data machine processable. The evolution of Semantic web from syntactic web has made data on the web machine processable and understandable. A more refined way to achieve this is Linked Data. Large volume of data is available in varied file formats different to RDF, known as Legacy Data. RDF provides a framework to achieve Linked Data. So, to publish these data as Linked Data we shall extract and convert them to RDF without loss of information. This Book, would try to explain the Linked Data technology stack and its working principles, highlighting some of its emblematic use Cases and implementations. This book intends to propose an approach to apply these principles on the bibliographic data Finally it concludes with comparison of used technique with an automatic conversion tool.

Mr. Vikas Bhushan, is a Ph.D. student at DRTC, Indian Statistical Institute, Bangalore. He completed his MS-LIS from Indian Statistical Institute, Bangalore in 2014. Prof. ARD Prasad (Head, DRTC) is a globally recognized expert in the Library science field. He has over 30 years of experience.

978-3-659-75594-1